Out of the Woods

Out of the Woods

Shaniese Armstrong

MAMA'S KITCHEN PRESS

Out of the Woods
© 2024 Shaniese Armstrong
ISBN: 979-8-9893829-7-2

Published by Mama's Kitchen Press
Austin, TX / Los Angeles, CA
mamaskitchenpress.com

First Trade Paperback Original Edition, 2024

Manufactured in the United States of America

Cover design & layout design by Emily Anne Evans

This book is dedicated to the social butterflies and the wall flowers. May you flourish and be kind to yourself.

Contents

PART ONE

Gremlin

Congrats, you have launched your human experience!

To begin, choose your personality:

A: The Dreamer

B: The Wanderer

C: Possum

Now that you have chosen your personality, choose your profession!

ERROR: Your mental is taxed %27 for every task you complete

A: Artist

B: Business Owner

C: Forest Ranger

ERROR: ALl Or nOtHiNG fEeLIng In yOUr boDy

ERROR: LaRgE pRODucTioN Of cOrTiSol

ERROR: LOW on dopAMIne

ERROR: MEMORY STORAGE LOW!

ERROR: %15 DAMAGE AT ALL TIMES!

BONUS: Side quests unlock

BONUS: Hobby expert

Character Complete!

Choose your companion!

A: Cat

B: Dog

C: Extrovert Human

ERROR: 1 companion capacity

Are you ready to start the game?

Skip Tutorial

I don't need a plan,

I have goals that I may work towards.

I don't know when or if I'll fall in love,

How or when I die isn't up to me.

Present gift wrapped in the art of doing,

In the perception of one's self.

Living in the past may lead to depression,

Living in the future may lead to anxiety,

Unfortunately, my brain likes to curate.

A cocktail of scenarios for both,

I skip what I'm supposed to be doing.

Hiking Trail

My inner guide's exuberant programing,
Takes the scenic route.
I take the trip you set me up with,
To prove I am naive.
Vague directions,
Face value functions,
I trust you to lead.
And yet I am the fool,
For believing in you.
I blame management.

Possum in a Coat

Focus,

Focus,

123

Focus,

Focus,

123

Pebble, rock, gem, crystal

That's a boulder.

123

Focus

5678

Now dance!

Change up the tempo,

Feel the breeze go with the wind.

Let your worries flow on by,

Photosynthesize the array of colorful rays.

FOCUS!

FOCUS!

123!

123!

Why is it so hard to focus on anything?

Focusing leads my mind to spring cleaning.

And the possum inside likes side quests.

Landfill

Passing thoughts and dwelled moments that
hold no semblance.
Runaway trains long forgotten,
Memories that should be important but got
chucked out with the useful information.
The blue tang fish touches every moment and
memory like it was never there,
Cleaning and sweeping my mind like a 9-5.
Some say it's protecting me, others say it's
hindering me.
I say I have no clue on what we are talking about.

Horrors of the Mind

Pain so exhausting I put it to bed.
Closed closets of skeletons,
Fingerprints wiped from the mirror.
I sit,
I lie,
Listening to the quiet.
The loud hum of the dryer,
The whirl of the fan,
The scribble of my pen on paper.
I am thankful for the break.
Even if today feels out of place,
The quiet sounds loud.
But I'll take the loud quiet,
Over the loudness in my head.

Ground Zero

You are my trigger event,

My insecurities are ground zero.

Primary silent explosion,

Chemical reaction freezes me in place.

The shockwave of complicated feelings,

Under pressure of my reaction.

Causing rapture of rage,

Debris of my buildings.

Acoustic wave of frustration,

I'm left with quarenary injuries.

Side Quests

Create Plan A,

Toss that plan.

Make B-F back-up plans,

Toss those out the window,

Then yourself,

Dust yourself off,

Follow that raccoon.

Watch the caterpillar grow.

Get stuck in a time loop,

Get unstuck from that time loop.

Realize that you missed the deadline,

Restart the plans you picked up.

10 Things I Love

1. The pitter-patter of the rain.
2. The warmth of the sun in the morning.
3. Dewy grass smell.
4. The raspiness of morning voices.
5. The breeze when it flows through the wind.
6. Intricate spider webs.
7. Walking.
8. People-watching from a distance.
9. The softness of moss.
10. The liveliness I feel when I experience these things.

Comfort

In fields where long grass sways and bends,

Blades whisper secrets to the breeze.

A sea of green where earth extends,

Their soft caress puts hearts at ease.

Beneath the sun, they stand so tall,

They dance with wind in joyous cheer.

Nature's carpet, free for all,

A wild symphony to hear.

A haven for the birds and bees,

In long grass, dreams find space to grow,

A world beneath the shady trees,

A timeless tale in endless flow.

PART 2

Photosynthesis

Frolicking in Sunflowers

When you feel like you can fit in everywhere and nowhere,
Come frolic in the chrysanthemums.
When you feel like you can no longer function in public,
Come dance in the tulips.
When you feel like your body is not your own,
Come lay under the willow tree.
When you feel the rush of euphoric energy,
Come bask in the sun.
When you feel like you are floaty in space,
Come frolic in the sunflowers.

Stump

Cut down to provide shelter,
Ancient stump stands tall.
Whispering tales of its past,
New life springs, grows strong.
From stump to sky,
Moss creeping in to take.
Whispers of growth deep within,
Nothing to stop the stump's development.
Life's journey takes root.

Creature of the Woods

Cool mist cascades down,
Over the tranquil terrain.
Nature's soft embrace,
Owls silently glide.
Through the moonlight's silent veil,
Hunting in the moon's glow.
Of mist and silent hunters,
Nature's nightly show.

I love the predictable nature,
The hierarchy of the woods.

Float

Above the heads,

Weightless in feeling.

I float here,

No pain or fear.

Sometimes I watch,

The body goes,

Control goes with it.

Where to go?

Palace to find,

Solace and peace.

I just float,

For what feels like eternity.

Pebbling

A small rock,

A little tidbit,

A shiny piece of life I give to you.

I will grow my collection to share with you.

A pebble to show my love,

Gratitude,

And attention,

Building the foundation of our relationship.

A large rant,

A passionate story,

An iridescent truth,

Share your collection with me.

So our foundation is stronger.

Holding Tight

The pressure of needing to be held,
Weighs down.
The restless of needing not to be touched,
Intense jitteriness.
A pendulum of extremes between both,
Never stand still.
Tucked tightly between weighted blankets,
Weigh me down.
I feel myself coming back to my body,
Serene feelings envelop me.

Greenery

A secret passage to the room,

Filled with eclectic furniture and knick-knacks.

2 sofas from the 1920s,

A chaise lounge,

A bay window with natural lighting.

A hidden bar,

A chandelier that has candle sticks.

A string of soft lights,

Bookshelves lining the walls.

Plants fill the room,

I want a green room.

Hello ERROR

Hello hindrance,

It's me again.

When are you going to stop being a hurdle?

At this point I'm just going to go under you,

I can, you are big enough.

Making me small,

Smaller,

Smaller,

Smaller till I cannot get out of the yard.

Battling with the ants,

Insects crowd me.

I feel as though I'm losing this battle,

Out on the lawn.

It feels this is my whole world,

Till I remember,

The world is bigger than just this patch of grass.

Cordyceps

The fungus has infiltrated my brain,

Causing irrational thoughts.

Just wanting to survive,

It thrives off my insecurities.

Using my muscle memory,

It wears my face as a mask.

Everyone can tell something is off,

Is it the pain in my eyes,

Being trapped in the confines of my mind?

I isolate myself to not infect others with this

deadly disease.

Sun Rise

Just to catch the sunrise,

I had to walk in the dark for a while.

The trail winding and uneven trail,

I made it.

Odd shapes in the mist,

As I come closer, it becomes clearer,

I have nothing to fear.

The dewy plants brush against me,

As if to greet me.

At the peak of this mountain,

I reflect on the journey it took.

I still have ways to go,

But for now I enjoy this Rise.

About the Author

I was born in Fontana, California
on January 20th, 2000. I love taking
walks to unwind, to think, to clear my
mind. Nature has been in many ways
inspiring to me. This is my second
book of poetry.

mamaskitchenpress.com

Mama's Kitchen Press believes that stories affirm our humanity. It is our mission to publish stories that are personal, heartfelt, and intimate.

youthwriterscamp.com

This book was created as part of Youth Writer's Camp, a program that follows a 10-Week Social-Emotional Curriculum promoting positive mental health, educational, and economic outcomes among youth.

The aim of Youth Writer's Camp is to:
· Teach adaptive social and emotion regulation skills
· Improve effective communication skills
· Increase literacy skills through creative written expression
· Empower youth by amplifying their voices to tell their stories
· Support each youth in becoming a published writer

.

Printed in the USA
CPSIA information can be obtained
at www.ICGtesting.com
CBHW051251151124
17428CB00007B/1162